Key Stage 2 LEARN

Living Things

Contents

AUTHOR: Camilla de la Bédoyère
EDITORIAL: Catherine de la Bédoyère, Quentin de la Bédoyère, John Bolt, Vicky Garrard, Kate Lawson, Sally MacGill, Julia Rolf, Lyndall Willis
DESIGN: Jen Bishop, Dave Jones, Colin Rudderham, Mike Spender
ILLUSTRATORS: David Benham, Sarah Wimperis
PRODUCTION: Chris Herbert, Claire Walker
Thanks also to Robert Walster

COMMISSIONING EDITOR: Polly Willis
PUBLISHER AND CREATIVE DIRECTOR: Nick Wells

3 book Pack ISBN 1-84451-052-2   Book ISBN 1-84451-034-4
6 book Pack ISBN 1-84451-066-2   Book ISBN 1-84451-084-0
First published in 2003

A copy of the CIP data for this book is available from the British Library upon request.

Created and produced by
FLAME TREE PUBLISHING
Crabtree Hall,
Crabtree Lane,
Fulham, London SW6 6TY
United Kingdom
www.flametreepublishing.com

Flame Tree Publishing is part of The Foundry Creative Media Co. Ltd.

© The Foundry Creative Media Co. Ltd, 2003

Printed in Croatia

Foreword

Sometimes when I am crossing the playground on my way to visit a primary school I pass young children playing at schools. There is always a stern authoritarian little teacher at the front laying down the law to the unruly group of children in the pretend class. This puzzles me a little because the school I am visiting is very far from being like the children's play. Where do they get this Victorian view of what school is like? Perhaps it's handed down from generation to generation through the genes. Certainly they don't get it from their primary school. Teachers today are more often found alongside their pupils, who are learning by actually doing things for themselves, rather than merely listening and obeying instructions.

Busy children, interested and involved in their classroom reflect what we know about how they learn. Of course they learn from teachers but most of all they learn from their experience of life and their life is spent both in and out of school. Indeed, if we compare the impact upon children of even the finest schools and teachers, we find that three or four times as great an impact is made by the reality of children's lives outside the school. That reality has the parent at the all important centre. No adult can have so much impact, for good or ill, as the young child's mother or father.

This book, and others in the series, are founded on the sure belief that the great majority of parents want to help their children grow and learn and that teachers are keen to support them. The days when parents were kept at arm's length from schools are long gone and over the years we have moved well beyond the white line painted on the playground across which no parent must pass without an appointment. Now parents move freely in and out of schools and very often are found in the classrooms backing up the teachers. Both sides of the partnership know how important it is that children should be challenged and stimulated both in and out of school.

Perhaps the most vital part of this book is where parents and children are encouraged to develop activities beyond those offered on the page. The more the children explore and use the ideas and techniques we want them to learn, the more they will make new knowledge of their very own. It's not just getting the right answer, it's growing as a person through gaining skill in action and not only in books. The best way to learn is to live.

I remember reading a story to a group of nine year old boys. The story was about soldiers and of course the boys, bloodthirsty as ever, were hanging on my every word. I came to the word khaki and I asked the group "What colour is khaki?" One boy was quick to answer. "Silver" he said, "It's silver." "Silver? I queried. "Yes," he said with absolute confidence, "silver, my Dad's car key is silver." Now I reckon I'm a pretty good teller of stories to children but when it came down to it, all my dramatic reading of a gripping story gave way immediately to the power of the boy's experience of life. That meant so much more to him, as it does to all children.

JOHN COE
General Secretary
National Association for Primary Education (NAPE).

NAPE was founded 23 years ago with the aim of improving the quality of teaching and learning in primary schools. The association brings together parents and teachers in partnership.

NAPE, Moulton College, Moulton, Northampton, NN3 7RR, Telephone: 01604 647 646 Web: www. nape.org.uk

Living Things is one of six books in the **Learn** series, which has been devised to help you support your child through Key Stage Two.

The National Curriculum gives teachers clear guidelines on what subjects should be studied in Science, and to what level. These guidelines have been used to form the content of both this book and **Materials & Physical Processes**, the second Science text in this series.

Each page contains exercises for your child to complete, an activity they can complete away from the book and **Parents Start Here** boxes to give you extra information and guidance. At the end of the book you will find a checklist of topics – you can use this to mark off each topic as it is mastered.

This book has been designed for children to work through alone; but it is recommended that you read the book first to acquaint yourself with the material it contains. Try to be at hand when your child is working with the book; your input is valuable. The influence science exerts on our society is increasing at an ever greater rate. Sadly, many parents feel that science is something they know little about – this book may help you overcome gaps in your own knowledge and thus be in a better position to teach your child.

Encourage good study habits in your child:

- Try to set aside a short time every day for studying. 10 to 20 minutes a day is plenty.
- Establish a quiet and comfortable environment for your child to work and suitable tools e.g. sharp pencils and good handwriting pens.
- Give your child access to drinking water whenever they work; research suggests this helps them perform better.
- Reward your child; plenty of praise for good work motivates children to succeed.
- Ensure your child eats a healthy diet, gets plenty of rest and lots of opportunity to play.

This book is intended to support your child in their school work. Sometimes children find particular topics hard to understand; discuss this with their teacher, who may be able to suggest alternative ways to help your child.

Top Tip!
If your child struggles with anything, don't worry – let them go at their own pace.

Parents Start Here...

Although genetics is not included in the National Curriculum for Science it is a topic that constantly appears in the press and on television, so be prepared for your child to ask you questions about it.

Life Processes

Living things are called organisms and they are made of cells.

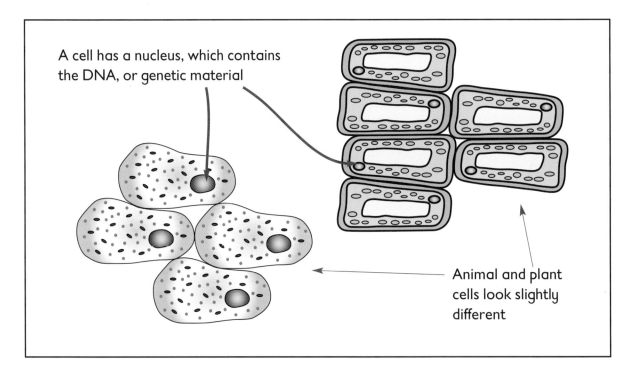

A cell has a nucleus, which contains the DNA, or genetic material

Animal and plant cells look slightly different

There are many types of living organism.
The two we are most familiar with are plants and animals.

Fungi (e.g. mushrooms, mould and toadstools) are neither animals or plants.

Organisms that were once alive,
but have now died, are also made of cells.
Things that have never lived are not made of cells.

All living things do the Seven Life Processes.

1. Move
   Plants move their leaves towards the light, animals move their whole bodies.

2. Nutrition
   Nutrition is food. Green plants make their food, animals eat food.

3. Excrete
   When an organism excretes it is getting rid of its waste. Plants get rid of the gas oxygen, we get rid of the gas carbon dioxide (and other stuff!).

4. Respire
   This means using the gases in air to turn food into energy.

5. Grow
   Big trees grow from little seedlings, people grow from babies.

6. Sensitive
   Organisms are aware of their surroundings and respond to them.

7. Reproduce
   All organisms produce offspring: plants make seeds, dogs make puppies.

Home Learn

Draw  around the things that are made of cells:

glass   wood   plastic   leather
bread   milk   diamond   blood

 ## Activity

Close the book and try to remember the Seven Life Processes.

Check Your Progress!
Life Processes
Turn to page 48 and put a tick next to what you have just learned.

Parents Start Here...

Top Tip! Don't worry if your child does not understand straightaway – children learn at different speeds.

Learning about how micro-organisms affect us helps children understand how diseases spread. Encourage good personal and kitchen hygiene.

Micro-Organisms

Micro-organisms are tiny living things. The prefix micro- means something that is so small it can only be seen with a microscope.

Some micro-organisms are only one cell big. Micro-organisms include living things like bacteria, viruses and some fungi.

Helpful Micro-Organisms
Bread and beer are made using yeast, a type of fungus. Yeast organisms have one cell each. They change sugar into alcohol and the gas carbon dioxide. This gas escapes from dough and the bread rises.

Bacteria are put into milk to turn it into yogurt. You can buy special drinks that contain 'friendly' bacteria. You have bacteria in your stomach that help to break down your food.

YOGURT

Amongst the most important of all micro-organisms are the ones that live in the soil. They turn dead plants and animals into nutrients, that help other organisms grow.

Harmful Micro-Organisms

Micro-organisms cause illnesses and diseases. The common cold is caused by viruses. Malaria is caused by a tiny one-celled animal and it kills more than one million people every year. Bacteria in your mouth eat the sugar on your teeth. They make acid, a strong chemical that causes tooth decay. Fungi and bacteria grow on food, making it rot or go off.

Some bacteria cause food poisoning. You cannot usually see micro-organisms on food so you have to be very careful to store and cook it properly.

Keeping Food Safe:
- Wash your hands before and after preparing food.
- Keep food covered so flies and micro-organisms cannot get to it.
- Keep food in a fridge. Separate raw and cooked foods.
- Heat food thoroughly.
- Do not eat food that is past its 'use by' dates.

Home Learn

1. Give one use of micro-organisms.

   _____

2. Name one disease caused by micro-organisms.

   _____

3. Why should you brush your teeth?

   _____

Activity

Look at the food in your fridge and see if you can find any items that are past their 'use by' date.

Check Your Progress!
Micro-Organisms
Turn to page 48 and put a tick next to what you have just learned.

Top Tip! Remember to give your child lots of praise – they'll work so much better.

Parents Start Here...

Biology is a practical subject. Get your child involved by growing their own plants at home. They can use them to conduct their own experiments.

The Structure Of Plants

Plants experience the Seven Life Processes that we talked about on page 5. Can you find them all on this diagram?

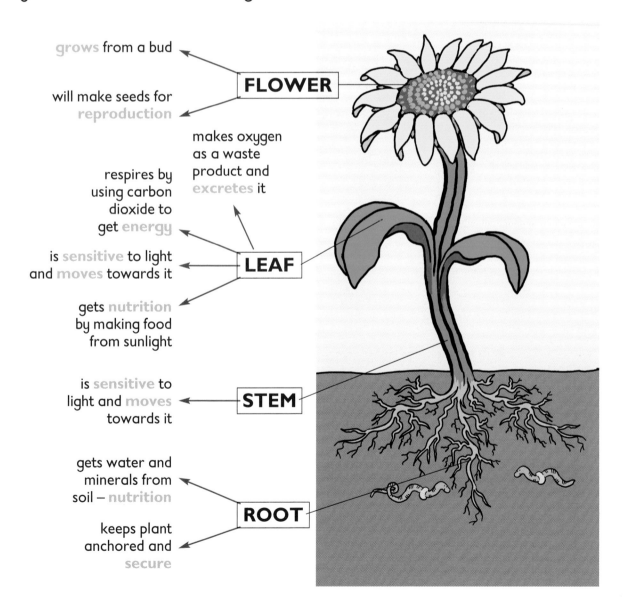

grows from a bud

will make seeds for reproduction

FLOWER

respires by using carbon dioxide to get energy

makes oxygen as a waste product and excretes it

is sensitive to light and moves towards it

LEAF

gets nutrition by making food from sunlight

is sensitive to light and moves towards it

STEM

gets water and minerals from soil – nutrition

keeps plant anchored and secure

ROOT

Look at these plants and put a tick next to the one that shows what really happened.

Home Learn

Label this picture with the four main parts of a plant.

a

b

c

d

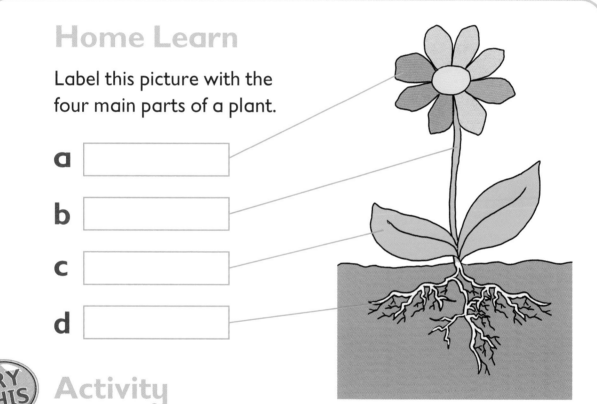

Activity

Start to grow a plant from a seed or a bulb. You should be able to find something that grows at this time of year. Get some advice from a local garden centre if necessary.

Check Your Progress!
The Structure Of Plants

Turn to page 48 and put a tick next to what you have just learned.

Parents Start Here...

Your child may have noticed that plants excrete oxygen – the gas that we need – and take in carbon dioxide – the gas we excrete. Talk to your child about how plants and animals need one another.

Photosynthesis

Have you ever wondered why plants are green?

- Plants are green because their cells contain a green substance called chlorophyll.
- Chlorophyll can perform an amazing trick. It uses light to turn carbon dioxide and water into food and oxygen.

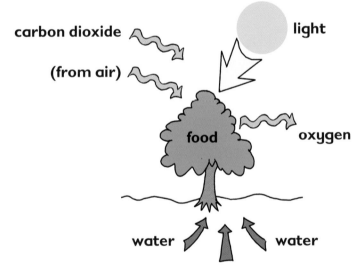

carbon dioxide

(from air)

light

food

oxygen

water   water

Carbon dioxide is a gas in the air. Plants breathe it in, animals breathe it out.

light + carbon dioxide + water → food + oxygen

The photo part of the word means light

Using light to make food is called photo synthesis

The synthesis part of the word means make

Remember: Plants do not eat food, or take it in through their roots. They make it using sunlight and carbon dioxide.

Minerals

A plant's roots absorb water. There are minerals in the water that help to keep the plant strong and healthy. Fertilisers are added to soil to keep them topped up with minerals.

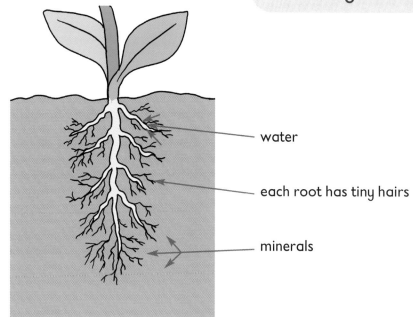

water

each root has tiny hairs

minerals

Minerals get into the soil naturally when dead things rot.

Home Learn

1. What is the green substance in plants called?

   _____

2. What is the name of the process for using light to make food?

   _____

3. What gas do plants excrete?

   _____

Activity

Put some cut white flowers, such as carnations, in a glass with water and a few drops of food colouring. Eventually the flower will turn the colour of the food colouring. This shows how the water is absorbed into the plant and travels up the stem. You can do this with sticks of celery too.

Check Your Progress!

Photosynthesis

Turn to page 48 and put a tick next to what you have just learned.

Parents Start Here...

Top Tip! If your child loses concentration here, let them take a break.

Your child will have heard about cloning on television. Describe to your child how clones are identical – just like the Spider Plant and its plantlets.

Reproduction In Plants

There are different ways that plants can make new plants. You may recognise this pot plant, which is commonly called a Spider Plant.

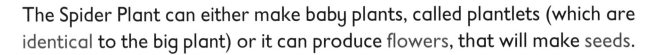

the plants produce baby plants which grow roots ⟶

The Spider Plant can either make baby plants, called plantlets (which are identical to the big plant) or it can produce flowers, that will make seeds.

Flowers are a great way to make new plants because they need two parent plants to make them. The new plants could get the best of both parents – just like you did!

Parts of a Flower

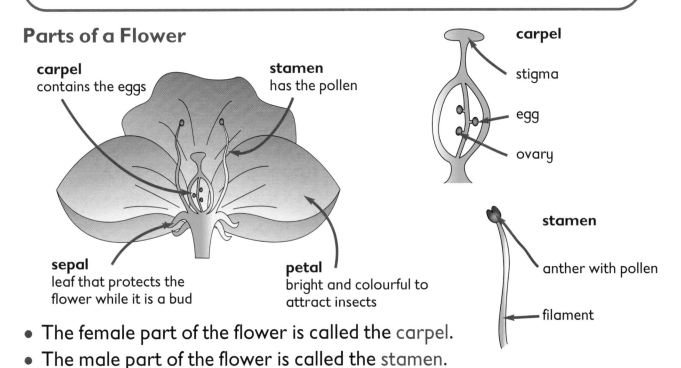

carpel
contains the eggs

stamen
has the pollen

sepal
leaf that protects the flower while it is a bud

petal
bright and colourful to attract insects

carpel

stigma

egg

ovary

stamen

anther with pollen

filament

- The female part of the flower is called the carpel.
- The male part of the flower is called the stamen.

Pollination

- A grain of pollen contains a male sex cell.
- Pollen gets carried to another flower's stigma by the wind or by an insect.
- This is called pollination.

the bee is attracted to the bright colour and scent

the bee comes to collect sweet nectar which it uses to make honey

Fertilisation

- The pollen grain grows a tube and the male sex cells travels down it until it reaches the egg in the ovary.
- The male sex cell and the egg join up together.
- This is called fertilisation.

Home Learn

1. Why do bees visit flowers?

   _____

2. What is fertilisation?

   _____

3. Name the female part of a flower.

   _____

Activity

Not all plants have flowers. Find out how pine trees reproduce. (You can do your research in a library or on the Internet.)

Check Your Progress!
Reproduction In Plants
Turn to page 48 and put a tick next to what you have just learned.

Top Tip!
Learning is fun, so if your child is tired, let them come back to this when they are fresh.

Parents Start Here...

Help your child dissect flowers at various stages of development. Point out the seeds in the fruit you eat.

Seeds And Fruit

Before a plant can make a seed two important things have to happen:
Pollination: pollen must get to the carpel (female part of the plant).
Fertilisation: the male sex cell and egg must join together.

Once fertilisation has taken place the joined male sex cell and egg can begin to grow into a seed.

Seed Dispersal

- The ovary grows into a fruit which will protect the seed.
- It is best if seeds are carried away from the parent plant, so they don't get crowded. This is called dispersal.
- Some fruits are tasty.

Look at this picture to work out why tasty fruits are good for seed dispersal:

Seeds can also be dispersed by the wind:

Seeds can also be carried away by animals. They have little hooks on them, or they are sticky, so they get stuck onto fur or skin.

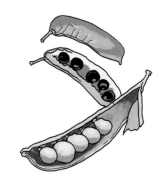

Fruits may also pop open as they dry out, shooting out the seeds.

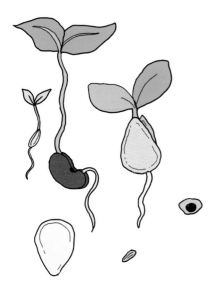

Germination

A seed begins to grow when the conditions are just right. Most seeds need water, warmth and air to grow. The seed cracks open and a root begins to grow first, then the shoot grows up towards the light.

Home Learn

Name the four ways seeds can be dispersed and give an example of each.

a) _____

b) _____

c) _____

d) _____

Activity

Take a flower apart and see if you can identify all its different parts. This activity is easier with big flowers, like lilies. Look at dying flowers, to see if there are any seeds growing inside the carpel.

Check Your Progress!
Seeds And Fruit

Turn to page 48 and put a tick next to what you have just learned.

Activities

1. Join the word to its meaning:

Petal

Male part of flower that contains pollen

Carpel

Brightly coloured part of flower

Anther

Joining of male sex cell and egg

Fertilisation

Leaves that protect flower bud

Sepal

Substances in soil that help plants grow

Minerals

Female part of flower

2.

a)   Complete:

  [   ] + carbon dioxide + [   ] =

b)   What is this process called?

  _____

  _____

3.   What three things will this seed need to germinate?

  _____

  _____

  _____

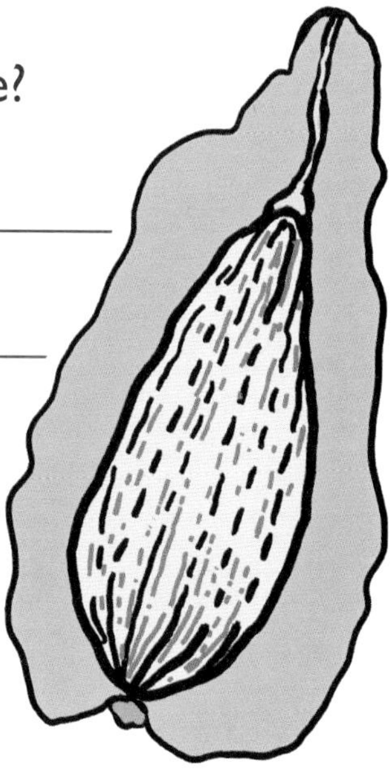

Top Tip! Bring what your child learns into everyday life – they'll remember it even better.

Parents Start Here...

Help your child set up an experiment to monitor their pulse rate before and after exercise. You will need a watch with a second hand, paper and pencil to record the data.

The Human Body: Organs

If you could look inside your own body you would find some very interesting bits – your organs. They all have special jobs and are necessary to make your body work properly.

BRAIN – controls your whole body. It does the thinking, remembering and deciding jobs for you. Your nerves carry messages to and from your brain.

LUNGS – breathe oxygen in and carbon dioxide out.

HEART – pumps blood around your body.

STOMACH – starts to break down food so your body can use it.

LIVER – controls chemicals in your body and helps us digest food.

KIDNEYS – cleans your blood and makes urine.

INTESTINES – break down food (digestion) and produce waste.

SKIN – controls your temperature, water levels, is sensitive and holds your insides in!

Skin is the largest organ of your body.

Heart and Lungs

Clench your fist – that is probably the size of your heart. Put your hand in the middle your chest and you will feel a hard bone. This bone is protecting your heart.

- Your heart has a very important job: it pumps blood around your body.
- Blood is carried in blood vessels, called arteries, veins and capillaries. Arteries carry blood to the organs, veins carry it back to the heart.
- Blood carries food and oxygen to all the body's cells and removes waste from them.

Look at the picture of organs to find the lungs.

- Lungs are large organs that breathe air in and out.
- Air contains oxygen – the gas we need to live.
- When air is in the lungs oxygen goes into the blood and carbon dioxide leaves the blood and goes in to the lungs. It is then breathed out.

> Smoking turns pink, healthy lungs black and causes cancer.

Home Learn

a) Arteries carry blood with oxygen to the organs. True/False
b) Food is carried around your body in the lungs. True/False
c) The kidneys control thinking and remembering. True/False
d) The intestines are involved in digestion. True/False

Activity

You can feel your heart beating by checking your pulse. See if you can feel yours: put your fingers on the inside of your wrist, just below the thumb.

Check Your Progress!
The Human Body: Organs
Turn to page 48 and put a tick next to what you have just learned.

Top Tip!
If your child struggles with anything, don't worry – let them go at their own pace.

Parents Start Here...

When children understand how complex and extraordinary their bodies are, they begin to take more care of them. Explain how bones are made from calcium, which we get from dairy products.

Skeletons And Muscles

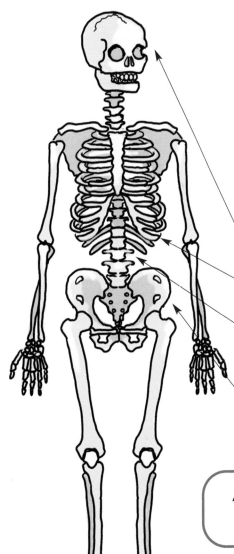

Bones

Your skeleton is made of bones.
They have several important jobs:

- Bones hold your body upright
- They protect your delicate organs
- They help you move

SKULL – protects your brain, eyes and ears.

RIBS – protect your lungs and heart.

BACKBONE – contains and protects the nerves that carry messages from your brain to your body.

PELVIS – protects your digestive organs and helps you move your legs.

A human adult has 206 bones in their body.
Bone is four times stronger than concrete.

Where two bones meet you get a joint.
Bend your arms, wrists and fingers and you will see lots of joints at work.

brain says 'move'!

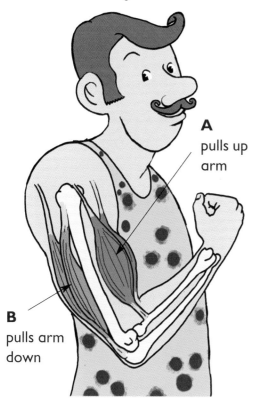

A
pulls up arm

B
pulls arm down

Muscles

Your skeleton is covered by more than 600 muscles, which help you move. Nearly half of your body weight is made up of muscles.

- Muscles are connected to bones by tendons.
- When you want to move your arm your brain sends a message to your muscles here (A), telling them to 'pull' and this lifts the bone.
- When you want to put your arm back again your brain sends another message to the muscles here (B) telling them to 'pull' so your arm moves down.

Home Learn

Complete the sentences:

a) The ribs protect the _lungs_ and the _heart_.
b) The brain is protected by the _skull_.
c) Muscles are controlled by your _brain_.

Activity

Bones are great at what they do because they are very light but very strong. How strong is a newspaper? That depends on its shape. Roll up a newspaper to make a column. Now it is bone-shaped the newspaper is much stronger than when it was flat.

Check Your Progress!
Skeletons And Muscles
Turn to page 48 and put a tick next to what you have just learned.

Parents Start Here...

How far you want to delve in to the subjects of reproduction and puberty is a decision you will need to make soon, if you haven't already. These subjects are covered in the National Curriculum and your child's teacher will probably contact parents before embarking on them in class.

Growth And Reproduction

Life Cycle of a Human

- Humans are created from just two cells. One cell (called an ovum or an egg) comes from the mother and one cell (called a sperm) comes from the father.

- The two cells join together and start to grow. Babies grow inside their mothers, in a special organ called the womb (or uterus). They grow for 9 months. This is called pregnancy.

- Once children have been born they change, grow and learn.

- At puberty children's bodies begin to change in preparation for adulthood.

- Adults continue to change as they get older.

- Eventually bodies get worn out, and they stop being able to make new cells to replace old or sick ones. That's when people die.

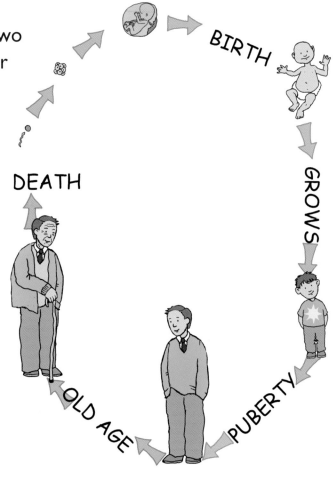

BIRTH

GROWS

PUBERTY

OLD AGE

DEATH

Who Am I?

You were created when a cell from your mother joined a cell from your father. Each of those cells contained all the information your body needed to start growing into you. That information is called DNA, or genetic material. You are special because no one else in whole world has got the same DNA as you – unless you are an identical twin (and that makes you even more special because twins are rare).

Look at yourself in the mirror.
Can you see things that are like your Mum, or things that are like your Dad?

Home Learn

a) How long is human pregnancy? _____

b) What is puberty? _____

c) Describe what you think would happen if no one ever died:

_____

_____

Activity

Do you remember when we looked at how plants reproduced? Flowering plants also had two cells that joined together. The joined cells grew into a seed rather than a baby. Look back at those pages to remind yourself.

Check Your Progress!
Growth And Reproduction
Turn to page 48 and put a tick next to what you have just learned.

Parents Start Here...

Children are expected to understand the function and basic structure of different types of teeth.

Teeth

Teeth
You have different types of teeth to help you break up the food in your mouth:

Our teeth are perfect for the food we eat – we have teeth to chew and tear meat and teeth to grind up vegetables or cereals. Dogs and cats have sharp fangs (long canines) that help them to catch their food and tear raw meat. Animals that eat grass have incisors to cut the grass and molars to grind it, but no tearing teeth.

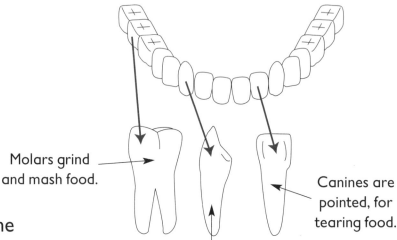

Molars grind and mash food.

Canines are pointed, for tearing food.

Incisors are sharp for biting and cutting food.

Looking after your Teeth
The outside of your tooth is covered in shiny enamel which protects the softer parts inside. Your teeth contain nerves. The enamel is very strong, and if we did not eat sugar our teeth would probably last us all our lives without causing any problems.

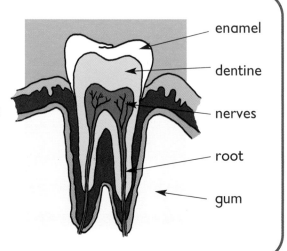

enamel

dentine

nerves

root

gum

What's wrong with sugar?

- The bacteria in our mouths eat sugar and make a sticky goo, called plaque, that they leave on our teeth.
- Plaque contains acid, which destroys the enamel and makes a hole. This is called tooth decay.
- If there is a big hole in your tooth then bacteria can get down to the nerves and KILL your tooth. And that HURTS.

> Honey, syrup, sucrose and glucose are all types of sugar.

Treat your Teeth with Love

1. Brush your teeth at least twice a day. Brush every surface of every tooth.
2. Change your toothbrush every three months and always use toothpaste.
3. Visit your dentist at least twice a year.
4. Use dental floss to get food out from between your teeth.
5. Eat sweets once or twice a week – maximum – then brush your teeth straight away.
6. Do not drink fizzy drinks – even sugar-free ones rot your teeth because the bubbles make acid!
7. Drink plenty of milk and water. Eat fruit and vegetables instead of junk food.
8. Throw away any cereals in your cupboard that are coated in sugar, honey or chocolate. Give your teeth a chance – choose breakfast cereals that have little or no sugar.

Home Learn

Write down three things you can do to prevent tooth decay.

1. _____ 2. _____ 3. _____

Activity

Look at the 'Ingredients' listed on the packets of food you eat. Sugar will be listed as 'sugar', 'sucrose' or 'glucose'.
The quantity of sugar will be given – ask a grown up to explain these quantities to you.

Check Your Progress!

Teeth

Turn to page 48 and put a tick next to what you have just learned.

Parents Start Here...

If your child does not like eating certain food types remind them why their bodies need the food. Try a reward system, such as stars on a star chart, to encourage your child to sample new foods.

Healthy Eating

Have you heard the expression 'You are what you eat'? There is some truth in that expression. If you want a healthy body and mind you need to eat different types of foods. The range of foods we eat is called our diet.

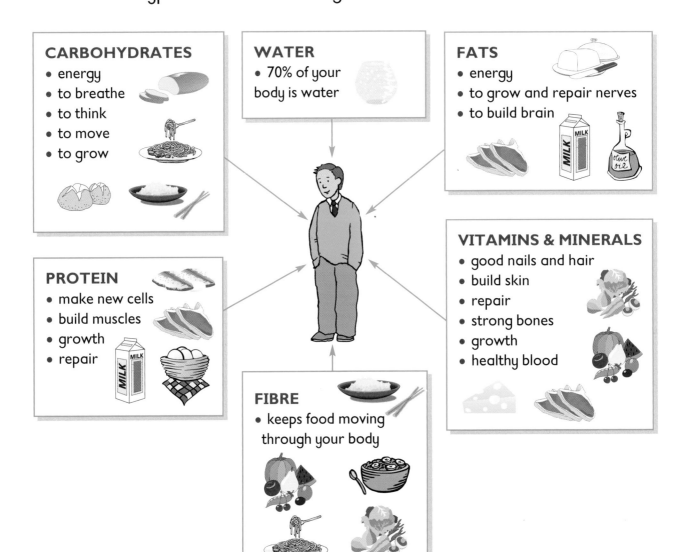

CARBOHYDRATES
- energy
- to breathe
- to think
- to move
- to grow

WATER
- 70% of your body is water

FATS
- energy
- to grow and repair nerves
- to build brain

PROTEIN
- make new cells
- build muscles
- growth
- repair

FIBRE
- keeps food moving through your body

VITAMINS & MINERALS
- good nails and hair
- build skin
- repair
- strong bones
- growth
- healthy blood

What happens to food when we eat?

1. You put food in your mouth, where your teeth and tongue mash it up into little bits that you swallow.

2. The food travels to your stomach, where strong chemicals (acids) break your food down into even smaller bits.

3. Some of the food passes through your stomach wall, into blood vessels.

4. The food continues into your intestines where more goodness and water are taken out. You pass the leftover bits out of your body, when you go to the toilet.

Sailors used to fall ill with scurvy, a disease that made their gums bleed and their hair fall out. Sailors got scurvy when they did not eat fresh fruit and vegetables.

Home Learn

Write the names of three food groups shown in the diagram and say what they do.

1. _____

2. _____

3. _____

Activity

Did you notice that we need vitamins and minerals in our diet? Look back in the book to find minerals mentioned somewhere else.

Check Your Progress!
Healthy Eating
Turn to page 48 and put a tick next to what you have just learned.

27

Top Tip! If your child loses concentration here, let them take a break.

Parents Start Here...

Your child's future health and wellbeing depends largely on the good habits of nutrition and exercise they develop now.

Living A Healthy Life

We have learnt that eating a nutritious diet will keep our bodies healthy and fit for life. There are other things we can do to look after our bodies:

Exercise

Exercise might sound dull, so swap it for play. That sounds better! All you have to do to keep fit is play! That means outside; in the park or garden. You can play ball games or running games, chasing, climbing or swinging. It's up to you. Walking is a great exercise for your bones. Your bones are made of calcium and walking helps your bones store the calcium in the best way to build strength. Sadly, twiddling your thumbs and forefingers in front of your game console does not count as exercise!

The best way to check whether any exercise is doing you good is to feel your pulse or check your heart. If your pulse is racing and your heart is thumping you're doing well.

Keep Clean

You need to wash your body every day, especially the bits that can get smelly. Bacteria live on your body: if you get very sweaty or dirty those bacteria will make you stink.

Stay away from the Bad Stuff:

- Smoking – you know it is bad for people's health and you probably hate smelling smoke around you. Smoking kills people because it blocks up their hearts and their arteries. It causes lung cancer. Cigarettes contain a drug called nicotine.

- Alcohol – your parents probably drink some alcohol. In small amounts alcohol (like wine or beer) is absolutely fine. But, like other drugs, alcohol can be addictive. This makes you want more and more of it. Lots of alcohol damages the skin, liver, kidneys and brain.

- Solvents – you may not believe this, but some kids sniff glue and paint to make them feel good. Sadly, it doesn't work and instead of making them feel good it can damage their brains or even kill them. It's a really stupid thing to do.

- Drugs – Sometimes teenagers and young adults take drugs. Drugs are addictive, can cause brain-damage or even death.

> Medicines and pills you have at home are all types of drug. They can heal people or make them feel better, but only if used properly. Never help yourself to medicines or pills, wherever you are.

Home Learn

Complete this sentence

I will never smoke cigarettes because _____

_____

Activity

Look in the newspaper for stories about drugs. People who take drugs sometimes steal money to pay for their drugs, so there are always stories in the paper about them.

Check Your Progress!
Living A Healthy Life
Turn to page 48 and put a tick next to what you have just learned.

Activities

1. Complete this word search

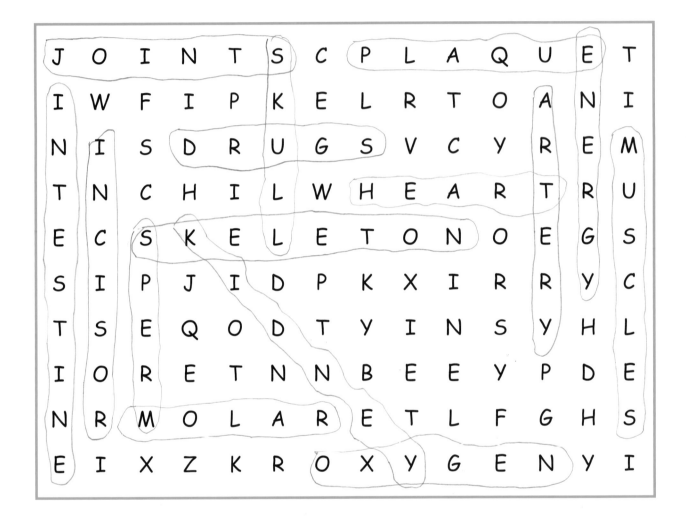

J	O	I	N	T	S	C	P	L	A	Q	U	E	T
I	W	F	I	P	K	E	L	R	T	O	A	N	I
N	I	S	D	R	U	G	S	V	C	Y	R	E	M
T	N	C	H	I	L	W	H	E	A	R	T	R	U
E	C	S	K	E	L	E	T	O	N	O	E	G	S
S	I	P	J	I	D	P	K	X	I	R	R	Y	C
T	S	E	Q	O	D	T	Y	I	N	S	Y	H	L
I	O	R	E	T	N	N	B	E	E	Y	P	D	E
N	R	M	O	L	A	R	E	T	L	F	G	H	S
E	I	X	Z	K	R	O	X	Y	G	E	N	Y	I

JOINTS	INCISOR	ENERGY
SKULL	MOLAR	KIDNEY
DRUGS	HEART	MUSCLES
SKELETON	ARTERY	INTESTINE
SPERM	PLAQUE	OXYGEN

2. Put ticks next to the three healthiest meals. Remember that meals should contain different types of food.

Plate A: contains lamb chops, new potatoes and peas. Glass of water.

Plate B: contains baked potatoes, chips and mashed potatoes. No drink.

Plate C: Noodles and vegetables with an apple on the side and glass of water.

Plate D: Toast and jam, bottle of fizzy pop.

Plate E: Spaghetti Bolognese with bowl of fruit salad. Glass of milk.

Plate F: cakes, crisps and biscuits. Glass of water.

3. What could Fred do to make himself healthier?

1 _____

2 _____

3 _____

4 _____

5 _____

Parents Start Here...

Talk to your child about the characteristics shared by the animals in groups. Reptiles, for example, have scaly skin and lay eggs, mammals give birth to live young and feed them with milk.

Identification And Classification Of Living Things

Draw (rings) around four groups of similar living things.

It is quite easy to group some animals because they look similar, or live similar lives.

Which group would you put a whale into?
You might choose the fish group, because whales look like fish and they live in the sea.
Or, you might choose the monkey group because whales are very clever, like monkeys and people.

When we put living things into groups we are sorting them out.

Classifying living things is another way of saying 'sorting living things into groups'.

Identification And Classification Of Living Things

Why do we sort animals and plants into groups?
- There are millions and millions of different types of living things on our planet and sorting them out is fun.
- Once we've got living things in groups we can give them names e.g. insects are animals that have six legs and no backbone.
- We have discovered that living things in the same group may have evolved from similar animals. Birds, for example, probably evolved from dinosaurs millions of years ago.

We can sort lots of living things using a chart like this:

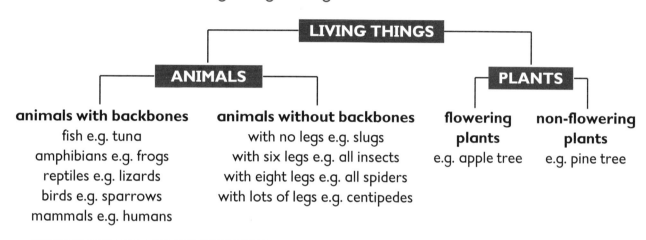

LIVING THINGS

ANIMALS

PLANTS

animals with backbones
fish e.g. tuna
amphibians e.g. frogs
reptiles e.g. lizards
birds e.g. sparrows
mammals e.g. humans

animals without backbones
with no legs e.g. slugs
with six legs e.g. all insects
with eight legs e.g. all spiders
with lots of legs e.g. centipedes

flowering plants
e.g. apple tree

non-flowering plants
e.g. pine tree

Home Learn

Draw a line from the animal to its group:

MAMMALS BIRDS FISH REPTILE INSECTS SPIDERS CENTIPEDES

Activity

Draw out some quick sketches of animals and plants and then challenge your friends to make groups out of them.

Check Your Progress!
Identification And Classification
Turn to page 48 and put a tick next to what you have just learned.

Top Tip!
Bring what your child learns into everyday life – they'll remember it even better.

Parents Start Here...

Some museums have collections of creatures that have been stored since Victorian times. If possible, take your child to view such a collection. They offer a good insight into how animals were catalogued when classification was in its infancy.

Using Keys

Identifying Living Things
Before we can decide which group to put a living thing into, we have to look at it carefully, like you did when you grouped the animals.

Look at this beetle and complete the boxes around it.

When we examine a living thing we can draw it and make notes about it. This often involves counting things.

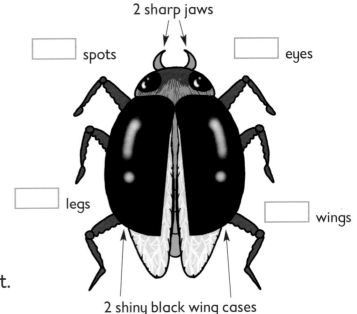

2 sharp jaws

☐ spots

☐ eyes

☐ legs

☐ wings

2 shiny black wing cases

What can you say about this animal?
Write your own notes around it.

Looking carefully at a living thing, like this, helps you identify it i.e. find out what it is. You may know what an elephant is, but supposing you had to find the name of a weird little yellow stripy creature like this:

You could use a key:

Using Keys to Identify Living Things

We can go through a series of questions which will help us decide what type of creature that bug is. These questions are called a key. Look back at the Chart of Living Things as we go through these questions. Cross out the wrong answer(s) each time.

Question One : Animal or Plant?

Question Two: Vertebrate or Invertebrate?

Question Three: Six legs, Eight legs, No legs or Lots of legs?

Question Four: Long, soft body or Round, hard body?

Question Five: Yellow stripes or orange spots?

Answer: This is an animal, an invertebrate, an insect, a fly and it has yellow stripes. Therefore it is a Yellow-Striped Fly.

Home Learn

Think about the animals you know to complete these sentences, using the words you are given.

REPTILE, MAMMAL, BIRD, INSECT

a) If it lays eggs and has feathers it must be a _____.

b) If it has fur it must be a _____.

c) If it has no backbone and has six legs it must be an _____.

d) If it lays eggs and has scaly skin it must be a _____.

 ## Activity

Find some living creatures or plants in your garden or at the park. Draw them and label them.

Check Your Progress!

Using Keys

Turn to page 48 and put a tick next to what you have just learned.

Parents Start Here...

Top Tip! If your child struggles with anything, don't worry – let them go at their own pace.

Discuss together how animals search, chase and catch their prey. Wildlife programmes on television often cover this subject.

What Animals Eat

Humans and pigs eat all sorts of food. We are omnivores.

 Cows, gorillas and rabbits only eat plant material. They are herbivores.

Think of two more herbivores.

_____   _____

Lions, komodo dragons and killer whales only eat other animals. They are carnivores.

Think of two more carnivores.

_____   _____

An animal that kills and eats other animals is known as a predator. The animal that is being killed is called the prey.

Think of another example of a predator and its prey.

prey

predator

_____   _____

Here are some other words you might find useful:
Carrion-eaters: animals that feed on other animals that have already died e.g. vultures, hyenas.
Birds of Prey: birds that attack and kill other animals or birds e.g. eagle, hawk.
Scavengers: Animals that eat whatever food they find lying around e.g. rats

Why do animals have to eat other animals?

- When we learned about plants we discovered that they make their own food using light, carbon dioxide and water. Animals cannot make their own food. They must eat food which gets digested in their bodies to release energy.

- Herbivores can get energy from plants. Unfortunately, there is not very much energy in plants, which is why herbivores spend most of their lives eating. They need lots and lots of food just to get a small amount of energy from it.

- Eating meat gives an animal lots and lots of energy. In fact, some snakes, like boa constrictors, can survive on just one meat meal a year.

- If you just ate grass, you would have to spend all day in a field munching away. Because you can get energy from other types of food, you have got time to go to school, the cinema, the park …

Home Learn

Complete these sentences:
a) An omnivore is an animal that eats _____.
b) An animal that eats plants is called a _____.
c) An animal that eats meat is called a _____.

Activity

a) Think about the fact that plants do not have to go off and look for food. Does that explain why they do not need legs, or arms, or eyes or ears?
b) Look back at the pages on teeth to remind yourself how diet affects the type of teeth an animal has.

Check Your Progress!
What Animals Eat
Turn to page 48 and put a tick next to what you have just learned.

Parents Start Here...

Look out for environmental stories in the papers to discuss with your child, particularly ones that demonstrate how affecting one part of a food web can have knock-on effects for other organisms.

Food Chains And Food Webs

We have learnt that animals eat animals and animals eat plants. We can draw this relationship.

A Food Chain

The pansy is eaten by the snail, which gets eaten by the thrush, which gets eaten by the hawk.

Look carefully at this picture. Can you see how the energy from the sun eventually gives the hawk energy to fly?

> A food chain shows us how energy is passed between living things.

sunlight
water
carbon dioxide

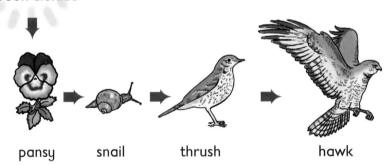

pansy   snail   thrush   hawk

Think about this
When the hawk dies its body will be eaten by bugs and micro-organisms in the soil. Nutrients from the hawk's body will return to the soil, and new plants can grow using those nutrients.

When we draw food chains we use two very useful words:

Producers: This is the name given to the living things that make food. Plants make food. In our food chain above, the pansy is the producer.

Consumers: This is the name given to the living things that eat producers or other consumers. ('Consume' means 'to eat'.) In our food chain opposite, the snail, thrush and hawk are all consumers. Food chains are very helpful when we are studying the animals and plants around us, because they show us what will happen if we change part of the food chain. Food chains connect together, to make a Food Web.

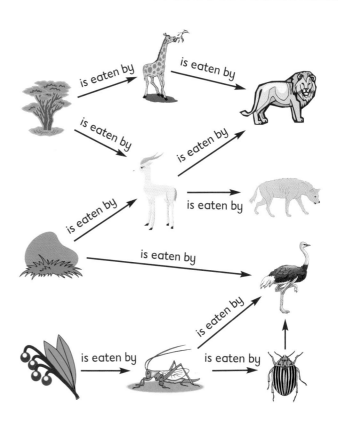

Home Learn

Mr Jones wrote to his favourite gardening programme:

I had a problem with slugs in my vegetable patch. I put down lots of slug pellets and all the slugs died, which was great. My vegetables are doing well. But I don't seem to have any birds visiting my garden any more. What can I do to get the birds back?

Explain to Mr Jones why the birds have gone, and what he could do to encourage them to return to his garden.

Activity

Look at the Food Web and see if you can identify the producers and consumers.

> ### Check Your Progress!
> ### Food Chains And Food Webs
> Turn to page 48 and put a tick next to what you have just learned.

Top Tip! Learning is fun, so if your child is tired, let them come back to this when they are fresh.

Parents Start Here...

Food Chains, Habitats and Adaptation are closely linked subjects that should not be looked at in isolation.

Habitats

A habitat is the type of place where an animal or plant lives.
Look at these animals and plants in their habitats. If you can think of any other organisms that could live in these habitats add them to the pictures.

Pond Habitat

Frog, dragonfly, duck weed, bulrushes, carp, water boatman, kingfisher

Woodland Habitat

Fox, rabbit, badger, foxgloves, bracken, grass snake, beetle

Desert Habitat

Camel, palm trees, scorpion, desert fox, dung beetle, cacti, snake

Habitats can be small places too: a meerkat lives in the desert, but makes its home in underground burrows. We can say the meerkat's habitat is an underground burrow, or the desert.

An animal's habitat may change during its life. A frog, for example, has two main habitats.

eggs

tadpoles

Frog spawn (eggs) and tadpoles need to stay in water all the time. Their habitat is a pond.

Adult frogs can breathe air and breathe in water. They need to keep their skins damp, so they never stray far from a moist habitat.

Some animals migrate, or travel long distances. They can change their habitats in search of food, water, warmer weather or mates.

Home Learn

Write a list of 8 organisms that live in or near the sea:

1 _____
2 _____
3 _____
4 _____
5 _____
6 _____
7 _____
8 _____

TRY THIS

Activity

Research the subject of migration. Find some examples of animals that migrate. Look on the Internet or the library.

Check Your Progress!

Habitats

Turn to page 48 and put a tick next to what you have just learned.

Top Tip!
If your child struggles with anything, don't worry – let them go at their own pace.

Parents Start Here...

Help your child to conduct the research suggested on these pages. Learning how and where to find information frees your child to explore topics that really interest them.

Adaptation

A fish is adapted to living in the sea because:

It has fins instead of arms and legs

It has a long, thin shape that travels through water easily

It has gills for taking oxygen out of water

It has scales rather than fur or feathers

Adaptations are special things about an organism that make it able to live well in its habitat.

If you look at any animal or plant you will be able to think of ways it is suited, or adapted, to its way of life.

A snake is adapted to life in a tree because it can slither along the branches.

An owl is suited to hunting at night because it has big eyes that can see very well.

A polar bear is suited to life in a snowy place because it is white and it can hide.

An antelope is suited to life on an African plain because it is a golden colour and blends in with the grass. It can also run away from lions quickly.

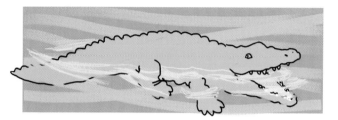

A crocodile is adapted to life in a river because it can hide under the water and watch for prey.

Do you remember learning about teeth?
We discovered that different animals have different teeth, depending on their diet. This is another example of adaptation.

Organisms that do not adapt to a change in their habitat will die. Sometimes this can lead to all of those types of organisms dying. The word for this is extinction.

Home Learn

1. How is a lion adapted for hunting? _____

2. How is a penguin adapted for swimming? _____

3. How is a crab adapted for fighting and catching things?

_____

Activity

Research the possible reasons for the extinction of dinosaurs. Can you find the names of any other extinct creatures?

Check Your Progress!

Adaptation

Turn to page 48 and put a tick next to what you have just learned.

43

Activities

Use this key to put in the correct names for the mystery beasts.

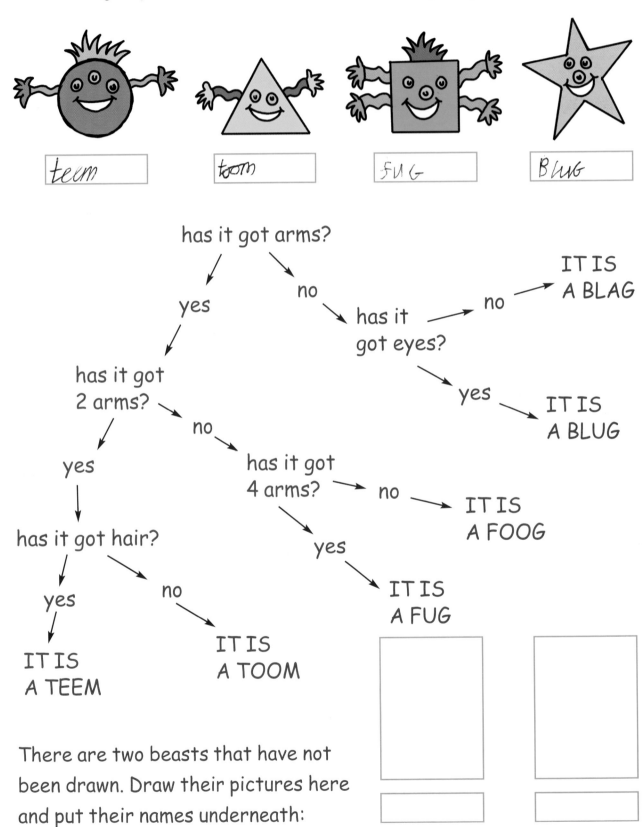

teem

toom

fug

Blug

has it got arms?

yes

no

has it got eyes?

no → IT IS A BLAG

yes → IT IS A BLUG

has it got 2 arms?

yes

no

has it got 4 arms?

no → IT IS A FOOG

yes → IT IS A FUG

has it got hair?

yes

no

IT IS A TEEM

IT IS A TOOM

There are two beasts that have not been drawn. Draw their pictures here and put their names underneath:

Follow the wiggly lines to join the animal up to its habitat.
You will see that just one tree can be a habitat for lots of animals.

Squirrel and dray in a tree

Badger and hole in roots of a tree.

Woodpecker to hole in a tree

Wasp and wasp nest hanging off a branch.

Woodlouse and rotting wood stump

Blackbird to a nest in a tree

Crossword

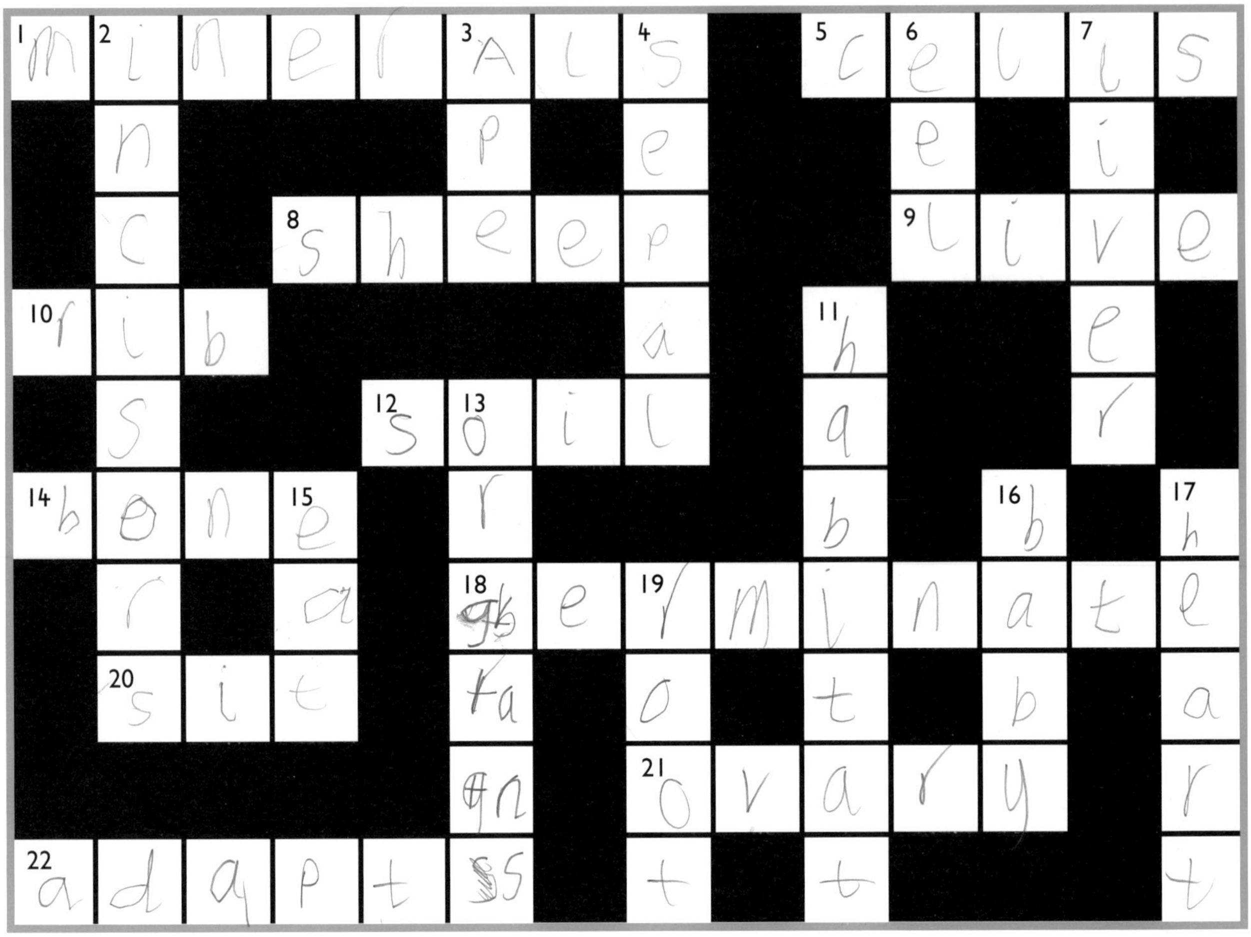

The crossword grid filled in with answers:

- 1 Across: MINERALS
- 5 Across: CELLS
- 8 Across: SHEEP
- 9 Across: LIVE
- 10 Across: RIB
- 12 Across: SOIL
- 14 Across: BONE
- 18 Across: GERMINATE
- 20 Across: SIT
- 21 Across: OVARY
- 22 Across: ADAPTS
- 2 Down: INCISORS
- 3 Down: APE
- 4 Down: SEPAL
- 6 Down: EEL
- 7 Down: LIVER
- 11 Down: HABITAT
- 13 Down: ORGANS
- 15 Down: EAT
- 16 Down: BABY
- 17 Down: HEART
- 19 Down: ROOT

Clues Across

1. Plant roots absorb these from the soil (8)
5. Every living thing is made of lots of these (5)
8. Herbivores that give us wool (5)
9. Animals _____ in their habitats (4)
10. Bones that protect the heart and lungs (3)
12. Roots grow in this (4)
14. Skeletons are made of this (4)
18. When seeds begin to grow they _____ (9)
20. We bend our knee joints to _____ down (3)
21. A place that contains eggs in plants, or animals (5)
22. We say a living thing changes, or _____ to its habitat (6)

Clues Down

2. A type of tooth that cuts and bites (8)
3. Another name for monkeys without tails (3)
4. Leaves that protect a bud (5)
6. Long, slithery fish (3)
7. An organ that controls chemicals (5)
11. The place an organism lives (7)
13. Stomach, kidney and intestines are all _____ (6)
15. How we get nutrition (3)
16. New person (4)
17. Organ that pumps blood (5)
19. Part of a plant that absorbs water (4)

Answers

Page 5 Home Learn
Wood, leather, bread, milk and blood are all made of cells.

Page 7 Home Learn
1. Yeast can be used to make beer and bread; micro-organisms cause dead things to decay and fertilise the soil; yoghurt is made using micro-organisms.
2. Colds, infections and diseases like malaria, Sars, HIV, cholera, typhoid, tuberculosis are all caused by micro-organisms.
3. You should brush your teeth to remove food; bacteria in your mouth that eat the food can rot your teeth.

Page 9
The plant moves towards the light.
Home Learn
a = flower
b = stem
c = leaf
d = root

Page 11 Home Learn
1. Chlorophyll
2. Photosynthesis
3. Oxygen

Page 13 Home Learn
1. Bees visit flowers to get the sweet nectar.
2. Fertilisation is the joining of the male sex cell and the female egg.
3. The female part of the flower is called the carpel.

Page 15 Home Learn
a) By wind e.g. dandelion.
b) By animals eating them e.g. berries and fruit.
c) By exploding open e.g. peas and laburnum.
d) By getting caught in fur e.g. burdock.

Pages 16–17
1. Petal
Brightly coloured part of flower
Carpel
Female part of flower
Anther
Male part of flower that contains pollen
Fertilisation
Joining of male sex cell and egg
Sepal
Leaves that protect flower bud
Minerals
Substances in soil that help plants grow

2. a) Sunlight + carbon dioxide + water = food + oxygen
b) Photosynthesis

3. Water, warmth and carbon dioxide.

Page 19 Home Learn
a) Arteries carry blood with oxygen to the organs. True
b) Food is carried around your body in the lungs. False
c) The kidneys control thinking and remembering. False
d) The intestines are involved in digestion. True

Page 21
a) The ribs protect the heart and the lungs.
b) The brain is protected by the skull.
c) Muscles are controlled by your brain.

Page 23 Home Learn
a) Nine months
b) The time when children's bodies changes in preparation to become adults.
c) The world would be very crowded but it could be quite interesting too; just think of all the fascinating people you could meet. Who would you choose to meet from the past?

Page 25 Home Learn
1. Your answer should include three suggestions from 'Treat your Teeth with Love'.

Page 27 Home Learn
Write the names of three food groups shown in the diagram and say what they do.
1. Carbohydrates: give you energy
2. Proteins: help you grow
3. Fats: for energy and growth
4. Fibre: keeps your intestines healthy
5. Vitamins and Minerals: for general health

Page 29 Home Learn
You should never smoke cigarettes because they contain an addictive drug, they make you smell, they give you heart and lung disease (including cancer) and they are a big waste of money!

Page 30–31

1.
```
J O I N T S C P L A Q U E T
I W F I P K E L R T O A N I
N I S D R U G S V C Y R E M
T N C H I L W H E A R T R U
E C S K E L E T O N O E G S
S I P J I D P K X I R R Y C
T S E Q O D T Y I N S Y H L
I O R E T N N B E E Y P D E
N R M O L A R E T L F G H S
E I X Z K R O X Y G E N Y I
```

2. Plates A, C and D are all healthy meals.
3. Fred should have a good bath or shower and put on some clean clothes. He should throw his cigarettes and beer away. Fred needs to lose some weight; he should take more exercise and eat a healthy diet.

Page 33 Home Learn
Snake — reptile
Trout — fish
House fly — insect
Tarantula — spider
Millipede — centipedes
Emu — bird
Cat — mammal

Page 35 Home Learn
a) If it lays eggs and has feathers it must be a bird.
b) If it has fur it must be a mammal.
c) If it has no backbone and has six legs it must be an insect.
d) If it lays eggs and has scaly skin it must be a reptile.

Page 37 Home Learn
a) An omnivore is an animal that eats all sorts of food.
b) An animal that eats plants is called a herbivore.
c) An animal that eats meat is called a carnivore.

Page 39 Home Learn
Mr Jones' birds have probably disappeared from his garden for two reasons. Firstly, slugs that have eaten slug pellets still look tasty to a bird; some birds may have eaten the poisoned slugs, and been poisoned themselves. Secondly, without any slugs to eat, birds will be visiting other gardens instead. Mr Jones needs to accept that slugs belong in his garden but he can control them without using poisons.

Page 41 Home Learn
Lots and lots of organisms live in or near the sea; these are just some suggestions: whales, sharks, octopuses, fish, sea anemones, plankton, seaweed, mussels, crabs, lobsters, barnacles, dolphins, whelks, oysters, sea cucumbers etc.

Page 43 Home Learn
1. A lion can run fast, it has good eyesight and hearing. It has powerful legs, sharp claws and teeth that are adapted for holding prey and tearing meat.
2. A penguin has short feathers that have a waxy coat to keep them waterproof. Their bodies are streamlined and their feet are big, like flippers.

3. Crabs have tough shells to protect their bodies. Their front legs are very large and have powerful pincers.

Pages 44–45

 Teem
 Toom
 Fug
 Blug

The two beasts that have not been drawn are a Blag and a Foog.

Page 46

Check Your Progress!

Life Processes .... ☐

Micro-Organisms .... ☐

The Structure Of Plants .... ☐

Photosynthesis .... ☐

Reproduction In Plants .... ☐

Seeds And Fruit .... ☐

The Human Body: Organs .... ☐

Skeletons And Muscles .... ☑

Growth And Reproduction .... ☐

Teeth .... ☐

Healthy Eating .... ☐

Living A Healthy Life .... ☐

Identification And Classification .... ☐

Using Keys .... ☐

What Animals Eat .... ☐

Food Chains And Food Webs .... ☐

Habitats .... ☐

Adaptation .... ☐